rummage

Advance Praise for *Rummage*

"I have been waiting for this book for a long time and I am *still* blown away by the shock of such an extraordinary new voice in the world of words and poems. Nothing can prepare a reader for the rigor and heart of Ife-Chudeni A. Oputa's *Rummage*. These poems wrangle with queer existence and desire in a way I haven't read before. How we rummage inside and with each other as a means of figuring out our bodies and place in the world. The love between women (erotic, familial, both at the same time) is deeply romantic in this book because it is also so hard, so impossible to express, and so often at odds with the world we live in. Gender is not a concept in this book. It is a living and changeable thing, and the reader must grapple with their own complicity in "rummaging" for a definition, a vessel to put the body into. I am a student of this book. I am reader and read."

—Gabrielle Calvocoressi, author of *Apocalyptic Swing: Poems* and *Rocket Fantastic: Poems*

rummage

poems

Ife-Chudeni A. Oputa

Published by Little A, New York
www.apub.com

Amazon, the Amazon logo, and Little A are trademarks of Amazon.com, Inc., or its affiliates.

ISBN-13: 9781503941984
ISBN-10: 1503941981

Cover design by Faceout Studio

Printed in the United States of America

CONTENTS

Lessons on the Body

All the Dead Call You Friend

Acknowledgments

About the Author

We Are Sitting Around
Discussing Our Shame

ODE TO SHAME

Forgive me all the years
I called you ash; I thought
you were a tree grown
inside me the way a girl
once told me a watermelon would
grow, if I swallowed the seed
and drank from her mouth,
my body already dirt. I thought
I'd swallowed you that day,
my mouth so accustomed to the shape
of a foreign tongue that your slight
tapered seed had gone down
unnoticed, or had been aspirated
as if you were my own
spit drawn down the wrong pipe,
where you sprouted and filled
the narrow channels of my bronchial
tree with new limbs, and tightened
my lungs the first of many times.
I thought you were my birthplace:
Fresno—your Spanish name translated to *ash*
in English from the Old English *æsc*,
closer in sound to the Latin *fraxinus*—
all of them meaning spear,
meaning my body is a wound
waiting to be made by you.
I've watched the canals in my city

fill with bodies in your name,
watched a man let his body wither
away to virus in your name, watched
a mother bury her child's body
in your name. Forgive me
what I have done in your name—
the speechless, invisible wounds,
for which some forgotten someone told me,
You should be ashamed. And I tried;
forgive my arrogance. I wanted
to be a weapon, a forest, a city that burns
one hundred degrees and more
and never turns to ash.

WE ARE SITTING AROUND
DISCUSSING OUR SHAME,

but I choose to talk about silence, and the air is still a metronome
of nods. We've already heard from half the room

and I am the only one dry—this is all anyone can handle of me:
nonjudgmental eyes and half honesty.

It comes around to you and everyone else turns a downward gaze,
but I make myself meet each glance. Your voice is a scuffed suede

that reminds me of being eight and playing *Oregon Trail*
with my godsister on my lap, both of us still

in our Sunday dresses. You are sharing a story I know,
but what I watch for is the familiar curve your chin follows,

the slight stumpiness of your fingers, their relaxed bend
out of sync with the anxious way you wave your hands.

When I see you later, heavy-lidded and drained,
I tell you how much you look like a friend—

What I mean to say is:

she was only two, and it was my hand
up her pretty ruffled skirt the first time

she learned to say *no*.

TUNNELS

Men made these walls,
cement curved like my back
against them. Her palm
flat to my chest. Lip to lip.

Young shame is a contagion,
chipped me into nigger-bitch,
kinderwhore, dirty girl/friend,
an erosion hidden in tunnels,

holding my breath 'til it passes.

ALL I REALLY NEED TO KNOW
I LEARNED IN KINDERGARTEN

I.

When you were five, you were bullied into loving a girl
who too was five and already a woman. She kept you off-
balance, knew which tricks would kindle your devotion,
make you doubt every pro-black, feminist slogan
your mother recited to you in lieu of a bedtime story.
She buckled you into a kind of need only she could soothe
with seldom acts of affection—her last M&M,
the gentle bob of her knee against yours.

II.

The same girl claimed your first kiss, her playground
flirtations sprouting wild while everything around you
succumbed to gravity and the muted colors of late October.
She took hold of your hand, led you to the mouth of a tunnel,
demanded you kiss her, then kissed you first. You'd never
remember if you'd wanted it, that or any other time,
but you'd remember that your bodies made a strange kind
of sense and you could sense that your bodies were made stranger.

III.

You were bullied into heartbreak before the age of six,
when her big brother called you *nigger* through a chain-link
fence, ordered you away from her like he too knew
you'd transgressed the limits of your bodies. And then it was her
warping your name as if her hands weren't still holding yours.

You'd learned by then not to tell all your young mouths had done,
so when your mother asked, you only let loose that word,
but she kneaded your buckled back just shy of straight
and set even the breaks she couldn't see pushing through the skin.
And you never thought to ask, to even wonder, who first
wrenched her into all that knowing.

KWANSABA FOR MY MOTHER

Tonight mother's Ford is a cell. She
speaks low. Her body no longer shifts
in the minivan, but tenses at his
cold touch under her Easter dress, lace
stained by trusted hands. Here, her pepper-
salted locs hang strange in girlish eyes.
My heart glows dark in our silence.

WHAT THE MUSE MIGHT SAY,
IF I LET HER SPEAK

Context makes all lines a little blurry.
Like how you insist on keeping me nameless

and I let you. I give a little give back
to the line between us, the slack wavering

your marionette song. Remember now,
I never led you to the mouth a second time;

you had already memorized the way.
You and I were still young;

we hadn't hardened yet.
But my tongue was sharp—

I'll admit that. I'll admit that
I needed something soft to remind me

I was soft, and you made it easy.
If you admit you aren't remembering it all,

you aren't remembering me whole.

after Geffrey Davis

PORTRAIT OF MEMORY WITH SHADOW

We played ring around the boy—
our shoulders crammed together,
his back rigid against the brick.
His mother took morning patrol
of the schoolyard, so we were careful to stretch
our necks into a canopy of laughs and lean in
until the boy could only crouch. He was no one's boy-
friend, not even when we took turns
slipping into the ring's center, so cramped
we had to straddle him
in the damp grass, our chests flat
against his. He learned obedience swiftly,
parted his lips and let us rummage.
The boy's spit tasted like any spit,
but he was sweet when we'd let him be,
his seven a little younger than ours.
His silent a little softer than ours, but
so much can be hidden behind the familiar
giggle of girls—even a boy. If we laughed
long enough? Yes, even we could
disappear into our mouths.

PORTRAIT OF MEMORY WITH DROUGHT

We were fourteen when the city declared an embargo on rain, shut off the valves, and drained the town—toilet bowls, water parks, birthing pools: anything too slick with wet. No one would name the threat, but we'd catch our parents whispering to each other about war. Some of the water went renegade, rushed through forgotten pipes and sprung up wherever the ground gave way—often in high schools and girls' bedrooms, where heels were already digging for a way out. Our classroom flooded, and Mr. L's algebra was annexed to isolation in a trailer at the far end of a dusty field. The walk there was long, longer on the way back, and sometimes we'd linger to avoid the dry noon heat. At night, we'd gird ourselves against the parched air and rub our faces with Vaseline. We'd walk miles to abandoned canals, creep past the caution tape and "Penalty for Looting" signs to collect fossils: mostly fragments of glass, unmatched shoes, the occasional bedpost, dulled blades, keys. Then, we'd load our bodies into tubs, packing our bounty around us, and soak in the substance of found things. We'd come to school bruised and chafed, with splinters embedded in our shins, badges of our transgressions. Girls had been taken away for less. But this is not why Mr. L asked me to stay behind that day. The floods kept coming. The city used the last of its assets to erect a water tower as tall as the Rockies to the east. I stopped scavenging for the solid, took instead to scooping water into jars I hid under the bed. I had seen what war made bloom in a man, could still feel the tip of the feather caress my feet until giggles turned to terror, see his fixed grin, hear him tell me how dismantled wings could unlock in the skin a hunger so vast it gorges itself, devours touch until everything turns to fire. All around the town, men strapped with vacuums sucked up guerrilla lakes and fed the liquid to the tower like sacrifice. Everywhere I looked I could see hunger creep into the corners of these men's mouths. I followed to rescue the droplets they missed, would gather whatever water I could. Found strands of hair and bits of bone in the absence left by every pool. I stacked jars under my bed. High enough to lift the mattress to the ceiling. I slept among the glass. They wanted to see the city on fire. I hoarded puddles like secrets. Trapped a tsunami under my bed. They fed girls to the tower like sacrifice. I gathered myself into glass. They set us all on fire. Cracked every jar. Unleashed a tsunami. We let the city drown.

WE ARE SITTING AROUND DISCUSSING MY SHAME,

though no one knows it. The night is a game
of Loaded Questions, and by the time I offer up
my favorite thing about my gender—
that no one can look at me and know
when I'm aroused—I have already arrived
hours late; I am already the youngest by years
and wearing my youth like a too-short skirt;
I have already mispronounced *coquette* like *cock*
sitting wrong in my mouth and stared too long
at the woman across from me, the tease
of pelvis above her jeans; my skin is already the tight,
goose-pimpled texture of embarrassment, and the truth
just slips out. I am everyone's favorite answer.
They are delighted with my shame. I win the round,
advance my game piece on the board, and am still in last place.

PORTRAIT OF MEMORY WITH EVOLUTION

The summer we lost our sight was the summer we learned what the seals already knew: that they could do more than spiral through the confining sea, that pinnipeds could be more foot than fin, could cleave to the land like sand crabs.

We had all been waiting for blindness, each of us thinning a different spot on our retinas, the membrane rubbed out, erased by friction, the darting eyes of the fearful.

The seals took to the land by daylight, barking and in droves, but no one noticed. No one noticed how low the shoreline, even at high tide. No one opened the schoolhouse to teach the children about displacement with an ocean of bathwater. Or evolution: how everything at the bottom of the sea grows legs eventually, or again.

We had locked ourselves away in mirrored boxes, a tiny aperture in one wall, a pinhole hideaway. A single entry and nowhere for the light to go, except in frantic leaps between glass and always stampeding into us.

All that light and we didn't see them coming.

The seals took up residence in our homes, passed themselves off as the missing: the limp-necked daughter, the mother who drove straight into the horizon—every house had at least one. Every house needed a happy ending badly enough to suspend disbelief, not to question why we now ate the meat raw and with our faces right down in the bowl.

We watched the seals take our places, watched them tucked in like us, made to whimper like us. We wanted a solution for night. We could always tell darkness, no matter how black, from blindness. Our eyes adjusted too quickly to the shadow's shadows, their familiar frames.

The seals tamped on to the next town. They couldn't take the quaint terrors of our homes, the way our absence matted in their fur.

We shattered the mirrored walls into glitter, let the slivers rip our retinas, scattering light— a flock retreating just beyond our periphery.

PORTRAIT OF MEMORY WITH NIGHT TERROR

We gathered the young and drove out to a carnival
three counties over. The children begged
for rides, to slick their fingers with sugar and grease,
to run free between the lights, and the beams that bent
with the weight of impermanence, but we hadn't come for fun.
We needed them to feel at home among the grotesque,
so we ushered them past the whorl to the sideshow.

On stage, the couple had our same glass eyes, same
velveteen skin—aged and ageless. The man
could have easily been a boy, the woman
a girl, we thought, given the right light. When he lifted
his arm and in one backhanded stroke painted
an eclipse across her face, her eye a darkened moon,
the crowd broke into applause, and the little ones laughed,
and we grinned along with them, our mouths stretched so wide
that the ground split open to its teeth.

WE ARE SITTING AROUND MY SHAME

or it is settling in around me—
one more metaphor of silent tongues.

This time let it be teeth—they can already hold
so much: wisdom and wishes and rot.

Let it be my teeth. Let them be aching
and ready for extraction. Let them not be teeth

at all; let them be engineers. Let them drill
through my jaw to my chest. Let them root

their way into my heart. Let them test the valves
and pistons and diagnose nothing. Let them find

nothing. Let there be nothing wrong with this heart.

*

What happens when you pull from the mouth its wisdom for
restraint and leave behind a hole that wants to be filled with
sound shrill and metallic and you are ether-hazy and tripping
on Vicodin and the room is small and small and smaller and
your father is there is not the threat is sharing the space that is
not enough and your gums hemorrhage and every swallowed
want you've logged on the ledger of your soft palate yet won't

admit threatens to leak out and stain your father's starched white cuffs?

> You rip open another and another bag of gauze; you stuff the wound dry.

PORTRAIT OF MEMORY WITH TRANSFIGURATION

The boy was a sleeping bear
at home on the floor
of someone else's home.
Home at my feet
drawn up into the quilt
like fur. His fur
delicate shards of porcelain.

The boy went to sleep a man.
I woke to a sleeping bear,
my feet wrapped tight in fur
in someone else's home.
Someone else's home wrapped
in the dying chill of winter.

I wasn't raised to keep bears in my home.

While I was asleep he was in my home.
While I was not asleep, he was.
I was half in my sleep and woke
to a light and a bear retreating beyond it.

The boy went to sleep a man and generous
and slept a bear and woke a man and
hungry in someone else's home.

I wasn't asleep and I wasn't at home
and I wasn't raised to tell men from bears.

In the light he was a bear
and in the dark.

Winter at its delicate edge
when the boy half woke a man,
a bear, and hungry.

I wasn't raised to sleep in the dark.

I wasn't raised to sleep in winter.

I wasn't raised to sleep bare.

Half in my sleep
my home was like someone
else's: cold smell of fur.

The boy, the bear, and
me in someone else's home and
winter dead when we woke.

In someone else's
home, I woke in the dark
and couldn't tell the boy
from the bear from the delicate
from the dead wrapped tight around me.

WE ARE MY SHAME

dropped into the silence
of a Mitsubishi—the sticky mess
of her and me, our union
hawked into your hand
as if to say, *Here, friend, a gift*:
the intricate mix of mucus
and spit clogged, until now,
in our throats, sometimes
running slowly the deep slopes
of our esophagi—clinging
as the unwanted are wont to do—
always, eventually, emptying into the gut
its nauseating torrent; yes, this
like the remnants of your own
terrors, which we have watched
thread silver through your hair,
rattle the base of your wrists,
start a whole hand trembling;
friend, you know the body's love
affair with death, you know what it is
to hold a cadaver heart
in your chest, its still
haunting, its power
collapsing the larynx every time
truth flutters up a heartbeat,
a crude resurrection,

a gift—this: our last drink poured
into your hands. Hold it;
don't let us slip through.

A Brief History of She

CREATION

A silver bowl, seedless white grapes,
swollen capsules that tang the senses,
wait, split and spoil molasses, tender
cradle, eggs held soft in mush until
the air is vermillion sparks, is dart
and linger, is frenzy sent like missives
on their wings.

NOCTURNE

It begins with the boy's hood
pulled around his face, while we
augur a new class of clouds,
warm breath quickly dissipating.

When does bad sense turn?
A flask to build a fire.
A flask to keep us bold.
Nothing to distract from the myth of nature.

Winter is somber with the promise of snow
and ash. We've been here before—
trying to sound north from the impossible echo of cicadas.
We are perpetrators of the worst kind of posturing.

Why haven't we learned yet—
that air this thin feeds on the lungs,
that sleep will find us choking, that night is no less menacing
when our hands are tensed in harmony with the moon and
 owlsong.

ANALOG

I held the boy's hand: kissed the girl: gave
him everything gummy inside of me: she
turned dandelion soft: he gave me sweet
cakes: I danced with the girl in a heat wave:
swallowed him whole: I drank her fragrance:
I mounted: his sapphire: her wide stretch:
the boy: the girl: once called me loose: spirit:
he held back: she took back: my grit: my
gleaming

ANALOG

Girl overheard: always running: mumble of
morning: wonder: prayed on the remnants
of: an approximation's approximation: girl
manifest: hours dressed in her face: deep
drag: fallen: girl on a journey: trail of fire
ants: always running: little marmalade: little
agbayun: sterile girl: speeding toward the
nonexistent: what you want: wanted: more

ANALOG

What brings the boy to liquefy sunset: what
brings the boy to seed: the boy a bled
harvest: what my hands have brought me:
whole: whole and full of holes this story:
wired to confess: break: bless: my padlock:
my egress: I offer none of this alchemy:
none of me

THERE—EVERY TEMPO

I can offer you
no keening,
but I would

apologize
for your lips'
moist sip of blue;

I'd dig up the hardwood
with the last shard
of whiskeyed glass,

and what I'd find
there—every tempo
approaching fracture,

every flaked-off
scale of sorrow—
I'd rebuild

into the shapes
our bodies
cut out of light

and distance, and yes,
this is something
like the active

darkness in love,
like slight, imperfect flesh
against the expanse

of a pin drop.

AFTER THE HOUR

:oo
I am thinking about thirst
[how strange to feel it
settle on the brain like ash]
when I should be making swift
work with my hands. Palm magic I brew,
deep tissue down the leather-delicate
skin of legs sluggish with years.

Lack is everywhere suddenly; I can see it
each day collecting in the thick pulp of the veins
I knead, the muscles a seizing wasteland.

And when all the bodies are gone from here
[none of them,
not one of them yours, none of them]
it colors even the window's silent offer
and the sun's whisper: *Here, here still.*

:10

We tonic for the tongue,
bitter wash of mollusks crushed
to coat; to melt a name into

well water and sweet dusk; to still a twist
of spine, its edges sharpened until skin breaks
and starts in on the shadows; to change shape—

glass blown to beast; to brawl
and churn sweat into a salve
for the waning light.

Every flicker grows weighty, waiting
for us to spread glitter-wild, while evening
swells in the mouth like a plea.

:20

this room's red is spoiling without the ocher of your skin, and
me stripped bare down
to the dark rings of nipple
you'd turn over in your mouth
my chest thrums with a quiver like
your touch gives, but violent
far from tenderness
us rumbles like ruin, and you aren't
enough to keep me waiting
in this kind of absence—too, too brittle

outside, you add up my hands. one to pull
at the curtain's seam. one to wrestle my bra
one to tap out trouble
on the bedpost
you've never lied;
sweetness has always pocked your tongue
and you've licked me to scarring
all I'm good for, anyway. but still my salt has
you counting down the minutes, hoping
for something like us to grow.

:30
What can you tell us
that we don't already know of thirst,
when even what we can keep from curdling
is spit out of the mouth like rot?

:40
How far does a voice carry when it is muffled

in the nape of a neck? How loud a promise
to kiss the listening backs of walls? Echo,

you uninvited spirit, was this your trick

of sound? Is dimpled plaster enough to distort
my lilt into another's round timbre? To reverberate

against the skin like touch? In the silence now,

there is no lip print on the glass but mine,
no scent in the sheets but mine, and her myth

fades into every darkening inch around me.

:50
A recipe:
Sorrow is a hollow root. Boil it in 2 cups water, ½ cup vinegar, and sweet wine to taste. The meat will go runny and sink to the bottom. Do not mix; let the separation stay. The slow odor of rust will raise a dizzying shiver. Do not wrap yourself in strangers; let the prickle on your skin stay. Take the tincture, still scalding from the stove, and dip in the ends of your hair. Let the locs drink until swollen, until the heat drips trails down your back. Gather the wet mess like a rag. Start at the window. Wipe down every surface; yes the curtains, yes the lampshade, yes your thighs and to the soles of your feet. Your head will be heavy, too heavy to welcome sleep. Let the weight anchor you to the floor for days, as many as it takes for each strand, full with the room's emptiness, to fall from the scalp. Wring the remaining liquid into a glass. What's left will be a drink mild enough to swallow.

after Renée Stout's Red Room at Five

SHE SHOWED ME MY MOUTH

then another's hands   needing only hands
without a mouth   the still-ticking face:
a clock   the face collapsed: a room
two tethered bodies   nothing
draws easy   lungs   steady panic
learned salt and breath   bristling
my mouth   then ate

after Sam Sax

ON THE EARLY ARRIVAL OF SPRING

I wore a suffocating sweater
and tall socks, unprepared

for the season's mild farewell.

You wore thinly stretched, patterned
tights, legs an accordion fold.

Something in your sheen there

made me want to pack up
her last set of earrings,

her shower cap,

her six-pack of grapefruit pop.
Made me remember

how good the glint of the strange can be

when you stumble
toward it. When you look on

without stopping—

PAPER JAR

She
    placed her
thumb
    in the shoal
        of my collar
    called me
            beautiful
        heart
    break beats
billowing
  from the streets
below
        She
    glass blown
        molten
            translucent
                I
    green stem
        freshly sprung
            wind wavering
        She
    drew in
    the space
behind my ear
  a paper jar
        filled it
    with breeze warm

peach plum breath
     I
wind-wavering
       crumpled

GIRL AS MATRYOSHKA DOLLS;
OR, A BRIEF HISTORY OF SHE

Here is the edge of a lake with no myth but our own,
where we balance on the bank, inappropriately dressed
for the cold and so close that the warmth between
us seems enough. It is darker than it is late: no moon appears.
We bring with us the evening's only light, lying
in the haze of low beams, car windows cracked to midwestern

mood music. We drink the glisten off her Mitsubishi
like champagne. The night hollows for us alone,
and we paint its landscape in our shadow. We're still lying
about what proximity can sustain, our nearness dressed
to look like what lasts. Soon, this bank will disappear
as our shivering bodies give in to the distance between.

*

My body gives in to sun, lighting the distance between
three days' discarded waste, a pile of unopened mail, ink pens strewn amid
bobby pins and dirty plastic forks. All my dishes have disappeared
along with the floor. This is an excess all my own.
My apartment is a pastiche of seasons, remixed with each undressing—
wool socks atop the heap that began in short-shorts and a lie

turning everything bitter on my tongue. I've been lying
here for weeks, my body a mourning sprawled between
drafts of a love poem, which remains unaddressed.

When I spot a Post-it she gave me, sitting in the middle
of the mess, I reach for it; I can't even do heartbreak on my own.
What I find is sun bleached, the edges worn, the ink disappeared.

*

I find myself—bleached, worn, almost disappeared—
the evening after she slams the door and leaves me laid
in its echo. I am a forgotten back-pocket dollar, the only
screw holding the light to the wall, the thin margin between
grief and ruin. I feel time fraying from the middle
of my hands, which are soon dressed

in its tangles. I am threadbare and undressed,
and in my nakedness, my body appears
a wax replica of itself—pallid, middling,
and nearly alive. Once-love, let me offer one more lie:
there's nothing left to grow this gulf between
us; no: *there's no version of this where we were better off alone.*

//

In this version, there is no alone; better
yet, she is still a night-stoop vision and my mouth
glitters with the secrets it shares: yellow maple leaves,
a body brought to life among the dying, how young
the lips at first *Oh*, tongue milk and gummy-
bear sweet—and too, how easily learned the posture

of submission, how easily passed to the next body, posted
like a gift unguarded among the trees—and too, how I am the better
for her, liquor and grab-ass all. Or was it that the words ran gummy,
stuck in my teeth like gristle, or that it was not my mouth,
or that she was a kind of wizardry and I was empty of my young
belief. Or that she empties me, takes even my fear when she leaves.

*

She empties me of fear and belief, leaves
only undeniable want, the thrill of an apostate
hunger, heart unlatched and suckling, a reflex of the young
and hasty. She is the shape of my horizon, my siren and better
since I was held by her and lived. My best days are a mouthful
of she as a recipe: rolled oats, butter, and sorghum

molasses—three shades of sugar and none too sweet. I go gump
for her, the memory of her, the scent I pray is her left
on parts of me she's never touched. What is a mouth
without her mouth. What is my waist, but her abandoned post.

What error of my judgment made her an absence, a lost bet,
the last wisp of heat from my waterlogged youth.

*

The last wisp of heat dissipates from the water. My young
skin softens almost to a paste, what's dead rubbing off gummy
in my hands—which is everything I try to make better,
which is all the things I can do without. The leftover
vibrations of someone else not alone shake the wall, poster
board thin. I can almost make out the contour of a mouth

pressing through plaster as if to invite me, mouthing
a word that looks like need, or mercy in the young
light of morning. I imagine it's her, posted
on the other side as a warning—all grimace and gums,
or a surrender—the sunk-back pose of relief,
of a love ready to give herself up for something better.

//

The first time she gives herself up, her gaze is a fog—
long, hot sigh on a fall-cooled window,
its instant evanescence. And then it is the bass
and scoop of a dance floor, the dark a thinly veiled
stare, constant, close enough to feel her lash
—that unremarkable vault of yen—on my cheek.

And then a long winter, still here. Still her, cheeks
chapped, shivering and coatless, behind the wall of fog
our breath makes—hot air, blown smoke, a tongue lashed
or tied. And then she is looking out a window
moving too swiftly down a road, and I am a bass-
deep pothole, the sky not yet unveiled.

*

My eyes now are potholes, unveiled
and empty, the lids weighting my cheek
with slack skin and shadow. A base
organ, the eye—always a doubled vision, fogged
and unfocused, dust-smeared window
into an upturned world, an image lashed

with tricks of light, thinning vitreous, an errant eyelash.
There is nothing but to let go the impossible game of sight, unveil
the unknown, its lightless beacon opaquing the window
as the brick. Now, I mistake everything for her cheek:

the door's wood grain, stove's open flame, fog
rolled in at the ankles, isolation's murmured bass.

*

She rolls in at the ankle and shakes my isolation to its base.
In an earthquake, tall buildings are subject to whiplash,
the highest floors vibrating to collapse, the debris a falling fog—
this is what I spend months trying to unveil,
and she thinks I'm being cheeky,
dismissive. Through the phone, I hear her close a window

and I miss the benevolence of wind, how
it always contends with the silence. *But at the base,*
at the lowest levels, the same buildings come out intact, undamaged.
Her cheek brushes the receiver as she turns her attention away to a loose lash,
the cat's gaze, some other sign of life that won't reach me in my vale
of dismantling phone wire and the low hum of barreling fog.

//

Ignore the wires, the barrel and hum, my thumbs cracked
with acrylic: I am trying to construct a name
for this dream that recurs, is different each time. Tonight
it is paper thin and torn against a blade's edge—the kind
I once slid down my tongue for sweetness, not
noticing my taste buds' bloom. It's a mosaic, a girl

unmade and rattling inside the memory of myself as a girl.
When I call out, she slips through early morning's cracks,
echoes like the hollow of another's throat, though she is not.
I want to fashion her out of angles and airspeed into a name
I know will return each time I release her from my mouth, a kind
of wind floating back to me through the long-stilled night.

*

Wind floats her back to me; the still night
gone, like the tear ducts I locked in her grip. A girl
dried out and beautiful and unkind
so long ago, when I was a laughter cracked
beneath her and she an absent sadness, an unnamed
haunt, the specter of every discomfort not

dropped into our mothers' always-open hands. What was she not
weeping for—her gravel-split knees, the burnt-out night,
maybe. How could I know? I can't even recall her name
or why I loved her. She must have been a different lover, not

that girl. Though, I once watched her undress from her body—a crack,
and every cell flaked into a spark, a new kindling.

*

Every cell flakes a spark. There is no kindling
like a body bared. I say nakedness offends me, then unknot
myself while she watches. She is a kaleidoscope, a crackle
of screen light, then fizzle. We go on like this each night:
reckless dismantling of silence. I sing a song of six girls
squawking like gulls on fire. She hears six ways to remain nameless.

I button together the leftovers: pieces of a windpipe, a name
discarded like a vice, singed gull feathers—a plume for each kind
of perfume stained into me—all of it smells of her. Every girl:
her. This is what it all comes down to. I have no more need for not,
night,
crackle.

//

Every cell sparks a new kindling.
You float back like wind, and still the night's
a live wire, a barreling hum, the crack

of isolation rolling in at the ankle. Shake a base
deeply enough, the holes are unveiled.
Give yourself up, you become as a fog,

as the last wisp of heat from water. A youthful
belief when emptied of its fear leaves
this: a version of you not as loneliness, but better—

found. Unbleached, unworn, reappeared.
You are the body let go from distance. Between
here and the edge, nothing—a new myth all your own.

Lessons on the Body

CONTACT

Somewhere on a street
something sleeps

small and leggy
against an unfamiliar

warmth—the back
of a knee, the wiry

curl of pubic hair,
the outline of a bottom

lip. Something small
sleeps sound and soundless

against skin—tickle
of antennae

or thread-thin leg
turned twitch

in the thigh
of a dream,

turned nightmare:
eyelash army marching

the arc of a foot.
Somewhere—a sleeping bag,

bathtub, barstool,
couch—someone unknowing

is learning how not to be
alone. I unbutton

my nightshirt, slip
bra hook from eyelet,

arms from straps, legs
from black bikini cut. I crack

the screenless window and peel
back the sheets, sleep coverless,

hope to itch, to wake up stinging.

PATHOLOGY

To say it happens in suspension, in whatever resists the smug pull of lines
    the logistics of our breath, our bodies
    curling the space between us,

        the exact measure of force
        needed to crack the spine,

            how much stillness it takes to craft time

  to say it happens unaided, without sanction, would be untrue:

watch the axon

    (long after the spark
    has jumped to a new nerve)

        still reaching across the gap—

FLIGHT

These feet could never calligraph
the name of the girl perched each afternoon
on the playground's highest rail.

These feet could never swallow
the debris: bits of graveled voice,
hair kinks, wind-carried seed.

These feet were fast in their fear,
            [of her quilled hands]
            [of what wilderness brings]
the calloused bones clumsy, careless
where they let their weight fall.

These feet could lie like all limbs,
could mask distress in stillness,
could take a whole body down.

TRANSITION

The blur of each instant into the next; the slow,
spreading chill where a hand no longer rests;

the thinning thread of spit as lips part
from lips: nothing is discrete.

This shifting is not a solitary thing,
this splintering of a whole.

      *   *   *   *   *

A single ray of light passes through a prism's blade
and it is a million rays of light. It is a billion molecules

of *no*. A trillion atoms of *stay*—
                               and then it is not.

           *

Everything looks alien
when seen through another lens—

labyrinthine lattice of cells,
magnified scales.

Pull the eye back from the glass,
blink   let it come into focus.

TWILIGHT

                            aurora

               still born, still-

                                    dream

              ribbon of light-

                     less-

                 ness

          marry the gray

                  that traces

                         sight

                            in

                                             to

                                                 shadow

                                        stillborn

                                     seam

             the gaze

              its gray

                 imperative

                    bloodletting

                ribbon

              let bleed
          into
          stillborn

          inter-
                    rogative

     wh
        -at
        -ere

      the gray
               its

        still-
      light
    less

MEDITATION

Think of the limbs twisting and twisting
until the body is cocooned and burning.

Of the cocoon—how wings rip through, then leave. Think
of the wings displacing wind. Of the wind

chasing its tail in a funnel
from cloud to earth, how it tumbles,

breaks through windows and the oak of a rocking chair.
Think of the chair's curves, how it was cut to bending,

the wood scoured until hands could touch
without worry of splinters like teeth in the skin.

Think of the hands,
how they were once small

and smooth, how they curled
halfway around the calves of a mother.

Calves thick, almost
beautiful. The mother's eyes

like brandy from the glass she lifts to drink
again. Glass lying in wait to shatter.

Think of the rim of the glass, how it is kissed
to glint with spit,

with the heat of 2,730 degrees
in the deep of a furnace. Think how it once was sand,

miniscule and limitless, trapping ocean in
the infinite lacunae between its grains.

The ocean's waves pouring
into a throat until the lungs bloat,

until the eyes burst
capillaries like poppies,

until the hands go limp and float
like the bodies of strange fish. Think

of the hands of the hands of the hands,
how there is always blood

pooling in the fingertips,
how they must flex

to keep from turning purple,

from swelling with the metal and salt of it.
Think of purple spreading the sky like oil,

oil coating tongues like praise.
Praise, a fire in the bones, unhinging

joints until the body cannot stand
or open its mouth to scream.

BAPTISM

Keep the body three days in darkness.
the body is not whole
Drape the body at the breast.

Let the skin fall slack and cold.
the body is molasses rot
Supple the bones. Fold

down the ears. Seal the jaw.
the body is petrified blues
Stitch the eyelids to the brow.

Plug the nostrils with ginger root.
the body is splintered palm
Line the lungs with perfume.

Harvest the hairs. Drain out the gall.
the body is disrupted night
Listen for when the sea is not calm.

Carry the body to the lip of the tide.
the body is unfiltered sound
Bind the limbs with sea vines.

Rub sand where scars are found.
the body is mercurial glow
Lower the body down.

Watch the waves close.

Watch the vines float.

HOW NOT TO ITCH

Someone you don't know is dead,
and now here he is again,
an inching, a chigger in your side,

a midnight-glazed sting.
You have learned how not to itch

ink on the underside of skin,
how not to dredge up a boy's cool-
mud hands, smaller even than your own

firm grip on his wrist, guiding,
teaching him the rules of this:

your hide, his seek;
your bare feet dusty
against the bathroom floor, flat—

not like the jagged gravel
as it shifts beneath your heels

on this afternoon much too distant
for his hands to reach.
You have learned how slow

the pulse of grief beats.
Count it out now. Again,

again.

All the Dead Call You Friend

IF YOU'RE FEELING BLUE

for R and H

It is only an ocean's blue-red sheen that can rival
    gray matter splattered and chunked on coats still hung
      next to the bolted door. I know

      the curse a pulse can cull from lips, its linger and call
    still dripping on littered bits of you. Its breath, your lungs'
last litany, locked now in the hull of your chest. I know

this: a hard *k*'s crack is sexier than all
    the syllables in *culpability* flung
      like your name off a tongue. I know that only ocean glows

      like loaded barrels, that the meter of waves drowns. It
    drowns my feather-gut supplications. Curls
you down in cerulean and rust, its bawl slung low
    along the tide, somehow still and shimmering yet.

MOSAIC IN NINE LIVES

I.

The pearl-sized hole in my sister's arm is all that remains of our
    messy ritual
after she cuts and drains the perpetual blackhead that swelled in
    abscess
to the size of a golf ball. The muck that oozes out reeks, has been
    building
up beneath her skin for years, only a hint of it sputtering onto my
    thumbs
each time I tried to push the puss out like a sigh, my fingers not
    nimble enough
to coax the body of its secrets.

II.

When we are still young enough
    to find the same things wondrous,
        she teaches me to play dead. This is a drill

      we run: one of us going limp midsentence
    while the other runs for help or screams
until the dead one says *Stop.*

III.

The neck bone's connected to the head bone.
The head bone's connected to the jaw bone.

The jaw bone knows to lock down
when too much truth starts scratching.

IV.
I am twenty-three and it is spring, so
    I break open
           a new silence
                and pull
                    queer out
                like hair
                from the throat—

She is not surprised, says,
As a girl, I had a dream where we
were lovers; what else could that mean?

V.
A cocktail or two
and my sister is loose lipped
and earnest, pouts out stories
she's forgotten not to tell, will forget
she's told in the morning.

VI.
We are women. We land in New York for New Year's Eve. We
    walk down the airplane aisle and
        my sister goes limp.

VII.
My sister does not want to go
to the emergency room,
although she cannot zip her own shoes,
she cannot walk, she cannot stand.

We have not trained for this,
so I recite the blackout back
to her
    slumps in seat/eyes roll back/bottom lip slack/*hrrrr*

then to a flight attendant, two EMTs, our mother
    slumps in seat/eyes roll back/bottom lip slack/*hrrrr*

a nurse, another nurse, a doctor, our father
    slumps in seat/eyes roll back/bottom lip slack/*hrrrr hrrrr hrrrr*

The specialist shows us the blood clots
effloresced across her lungs like so many dandelion
seeds, so many unspoken things.

VIII.
The funny bone, though connected to the arm bone, is not a
bone at all. It is the nerve that—after days sleeping upright beside
my sister's bed, head heavy atop my right fist, elbow compressed
onto the corner of the armrest—radiates a warning down my
forearm telling my pinky and ring fingers to go numb, so that I
cannot hold a pen or bend my arm to write at all.

IX.
The body wants to be a private thing—this I understand:
there are things I still won't tell her, even when she asks.

THE PROPHET GETS IT WRONG

You are a half dream that visits me in waking
hours, soundless as the voice of God. And there
is no fire, the bush a leafless, splintered pew.

This sea is the wrong color for miracles, glints
plum with flecks of wine, dark spots from spit-up
and coffee stains; not even the blood is red.

This staff is just a stick. I know only the sinister
edge of transformation: the body's grave silence
is an unholy mass. Lucid reverie, you greeted me

like a kiss from a friend, then laced my gums
with spoiled portent. You made a liar out of me,
cheated me with the pretense of a death I'd own.

How slippery your whispered prophecy;
how quickly you gave another's body to the ground.

THE PROPHET TRIES TO EXPLAIN

She's not color.
She's gut.
Not the milky
glimmer of
pearl, but
a knowing blind—
yes, as death.
And just as easily
she's forgotten.

*

She will not come
in dreams. She will
not speak through
crystal. She'll
sit too close to you
on the bus. She'll
float into your iced
tea. She'll cough,
sigh. You'll think
she's just you.

*

You won't
want to

let her
go. But,
you will.
It's necessary
to knead down
the knowing
until you can lift
your tongue,
lift without her
weight—

dissolve
almost

THE PROPHET WANTS TO ATONE

"For God so loved the world . . ."
      —John 3:16

Ask me what it's like to be a world
always in need of rescue. A life raft

of palm fronds stitched together
by a thousand bees. Yes, the life

of a thousand bees is all it takes
to rescue a world. And the tree,

now gone from our south lawn,
where it bled milky white and sweet

all summer, arboreal stigmata. Like me
it bled, my white blood drawn out

red and too often and too much
still for infant veins. Ask me

how much a palm tree can stand
before bending to the wind

is not enough and it must break
down and let the gale carry it,

leaving not even a whisper faint as the evening's
echo of wings. Except in the way I suck back

my breath like my heart is fueled by carbon.
Ask me how long a carbon heart can last

before the blood turns black.
Sixteen years is not enough

to hone a world's ears to the low timbre of death;
I was bound to hear it wrong. Believe me,

this world would never ask for substitution. I have
always been content to make my own

atonement, to give myself over to the flame,
to make of myself a sweet aroma. The scent

of someone else sick with my suffering
is sour. Ask me what pieces of the dead remain

to keep a world from falling. It must be what rattles
just behind my voice when I let myself forget

how much of me does not belong to me;
when I start to ask myself what happens

when there is nothing left to give,
when I am all that is left to give?

ALL THE DEAD CALL YOU FRIEND

for Chinaka Hodge

The street is pitch and empty and still
not alone. Everything wants to give

itself to black. Watch the leaves unlearn
their photosynthesis, drink in the moon's

shadow like mercy. The asphalt
clothes itself in the tire tread's

darkened burn. You wear your eyes
like a veil of mourning, pupils in total eclipse:

black open to black: prayer of equilibrium.
Prayer of wind-swelled body. Prayer of hours

tendered like grace. The star-silent sky
is not a harbinger. The night is not a shroud;

it is the song you lull in the absence,
the low chorus that answers you back.

ACKNOWLEDGMENTS

Thank you to the editors of the following publications, where the poems listed first appeared (sometimes in alternate forms):

- *[Pank]*: "After the Hour"
- *Callaloo*: "Mosaic in Nine Lives," "Portrait of Memory with Shadow," "We are sitting around discussing our shame"
- *Crab Orchard Review*: "Portrait of Memory with Drought"
- *Gabby*: "We are my shame"
- *Muzzle*: "Baptism"
- *Nepantla*: "How Not to Itch"
- *The Offing*: "She showed me my mouth"

Thank you to Jericho Brown, Cornelius Eady, and Kimiko Hahn for selecting this book for the Little A Poetry Contest.

Thank you to Morgan Parker for her voice in this world and her hand in this book.

Thank you to Cave Canem, Lambda Literary, and the Callaloo Creative Writing Workshop.

Thank you to the countless teachers without whom this book would not exist, especially Lee Herrick, Tony Medina, Catherine

Bowman, Debra Kang Dean, Margaret Ronda, Adrian Matejka, Vievee Francis, Gregory Pardlo, Lyrae Van Clief-Stefanon, Patricia Smith, Chris Abani, and Toi Derricotte.

Thank you to the friends and colleagues who directly and indirectly shaped these poems, especially Cate Lycurgus, Keith Leonard, Jennifer Leonard, Michael Mlekoday, Nicole Lawrence, Kien Lam, Chinaka Hodge, Nia I'man Smith, and Candice Iloh.

Special thanks to Scott Fenton and Doug Paul Case for shelter, celebration, and encouragement.

Thank you to Holly Mayne for your relentless love and support.

Thank you to Nandi Comer for riding shotgun on this continued journey.

Thank you to Tia Clark for being my ace.

Thank you to Ross Gay for mentorship, friendship, and my growing appreciation for bees.

To my mother, father, and sisters—*thank you* doesn't begin to scratch the surface.

ABOUT THE AUTHOR

Ife-Chudeni A. Oputa is a Cave Canem, *Callaloo*, and Lambda Literary fellow. Her poetry and prose have appeared or are forthcoming in *Matter, Some Call It Ballin', Gabby*, the *Los Angeles Review of Books*, and elsewhere. She is a native of Fresno, California.